Leading your

Marriage into the

Promised Land

Dr. Derrick L. Campbell

For Ray & Melya,
God loves both of you,
Dr. Derrick L. Campbell

All scriptures included and referred to in the text
are from the King James translation of the Holy
Bible.

DLC Consultant Group
PO Box 1668
Blackwood, New Jersey 08012
Visit our website @
www.dlconsultantgroup.com

First edition: February 2009

ISBN: 978-0-9802039-4-3

Library of Congress Control Number:
2009900300

Printed in the United States of America

FOREWORD

I am so excited about this book. *Leading Your Marriage into the Promised Land* was birthed out of a situation that caused great pain for Derrick and I in our marriage. But God is faithful. Just like when a woman is going through labor – it can be difficult to believe that at the end of the birthing process there's going to be a beautiful baby who will grow into a mature adult and become someone whom God can use for His purpose. So it was during our time of struggle in our marriage.

When Derrick led me through our tough times using the tools that he writes about in this book, I experienced a great sense of joy. For the first time in our marriage we were communicating on a level where we both felt safe in expressing our different values and beliefs.

Leading Your Marriage into the Promised Land provides husbands with the tools necessary to successfully lead their marriage. I pray that you and your spouse will embrace the leadership techniques taught in this book and allow God to lead you into your promised land where there is an abundance of milk and honey flowing freely.

To my husband ... You are a tremendous man of God, and every time I watch God unleash the greatness that is on the inside of you, I am reminded of what a blessed woman I am for knowing you and sharing in the covenant of marriage with you.

Sheila Campbell

PREFACE

This is not a book about marriage counseling – nor is this a book that will diagnose marital problems and then suggest solutions. This is a book about leadership. This book educates men on a process for successfully leading their marriage.

The idea for writing *Leading Your Marriage into the Promised Land* originated from a marital problem that my wife and I were facing, which could have resulted in a divorce. The challenge I faced was how I was going to keep my marriage blessed and fruitful while avoiding the continuing disagreements we found ourselves trapped in, that always resulted in blaming one another for the problem. A greater concern was that I knew my wife well; she is a strong–willed, intelligent woman. So, how was I going to lead my wife in such a manner that was not only acceptable to both of us but that also glorified God?

Leading Your Marriage into the Promised Land educates the husband on a leadership process that ensures the husband and wife develops family goals together, as a team. These goals must embrace the different values each has learned since childhood, since those values influence their perceptions of the different roles for the husband and wife.

Leading Your Marriage into the Promised Land includes six chapters and an appendix. Chapter one provides a brief history of marriage by reviewing the role of the husband and wife from the beginning of biblical times to the present time. The chapter continues with the societal influences on marriage and God's intent for marriage. In chapter two I define and discuss the five different organizational defensive levels that influence marriages. Chapter three provides a closer look at the advantages of teamwork for husbands and wives and concludes with a communication activity for husbands. In chapter four I discuss the term *shared vision* and provide biblical examples for its usage. Chapter five includes the entire leadership process. During the process, the husband and wife develop a shared vision and work as a team to develop and expand spiritual, family, social, educational, physical, employment/work, recreation/fun, and financial goals. Also in Chapter 5 the husband and wife construct a timeline and budget for the goals they've developed together. Chapter 6 is a brief summary. The appendix includes a step-by-step outline of the leadership process in table format and scriptures that were referenced in the text but not expanded on.

All scriptures included and referred to in the text are from the King James translation of the Holy Bible, and those that are bolded are direct quotes from Jesus Christ.

ACKNOWLEDGMENTS

First I would like to give God – the Father of Jesus Christ – all of the praise and honor. Without Him this book would not have been possible.

I would also like to acknowledge my wife, Sheila, for participating in the process, which resulted in the different transformation strategies I learned in the process of completing my doctorate degree. I would also like to acknowledge my wife's friend Carol, who reminded me of the need for making this process available to present and future husbands.

CONTENTS

YOUR PROMISED LAND

Since the ascension of Jesus Christ into heaven, the world's changing social and economic systems have had an impact on the family and the roles of the husband and the wife.

The history of marriage in Western civilization has its roots in the Ancient Greek, Roman, German, and Hebrew cultures. In Ancient Greece, the father arranged the marriage with a signed contract. Normally, the groom was in his thirties, while the bride was a teenager. There was also a disparity in equality and education. Ancient Greek society considered women inferior. Women were confined to the home and their primary functions were to produce children and manage the household, while husbands were responsible for public affairs.

Early in Roman history, the husband had the authority to punish, sell, or kill his wife or children. Eventually, women gained increased control over their lives and property. The authority of the Roman husband is in stark contrast to that of an Israelite husband. Early in Israel's history the primary purpose of the wife was to reproduce a male who would receive the family inheritance. It was the responsibility of the husband to care for and provide for his family.

In today's world, the purpose of the wife has evolved. Many wives have equal responsibility for contributing to the household finances by working daily. They also care for their children and husband, as well as perform other duties. These new values influence the Christian home and ultimately influence the relationship between the Christian man and his wife.

There are also many other influences that exist in the world that can make it difficult for a Christian man or woman who desires to have a marriage based on the principles that exist in the Word of God. Those influences are shaped by societal values that tend to embrace same sex marriages, open marriages, and divorce for any reason. The scriptures clearly define marriage as a relationship between one man and one woman.

God reveals in Genesis 2:24 that the original intent for marriage was that it be a permanent relationship between one man and one woman.

> *Therefore a man shall leave his father and mother and be joined to his wife, and they shall become one flesh. (Genesis 2:24, KJV)*

Marriage is a major adjustment for men and for women. The man must embark on a monumental shift in thinking. While under the care of his father and mother, he was permitted and encouraged to operate independently while interacting interdependently with his siblings. During this time, his love was expressed towards his family members.

Once married, the scriptures direct him to focus his love on his wife.

> *This is a great mystery, but I speak concerning Christ and the church. Nevertheless, let each one of you in particular so love his own wife as himself, and let the wife see that she respects her husband. (Ephesians 5:32-33, KJV)*

The husband must now learn to become the

leader of his wife and family. He must love and lead his wife as Christ loves and leads the Church. However, the different values that the husband and wife bring to the marriage can present many challenges.

This requires the husband to take on a leadership style that will foster respect for both partners' values and roles in the marriage.

When a man does not utilize appropriate leadership strategies, the result can be a disconnection between himself and his wife emotionally, physically, and spiritually, and then possibly separation and divorce. Divorce is in direct opposition to God's intent and design for marriage, which is that it be an unconditional lifetime commitment between a man and a woman, a covenant that is supported by scripture. Jesus emphasized God's intention that marriage be a lifetime commitment in Matthew 19:4-9 and Mark 10:5-9.

> *And He answered and said to them,* *Have you not read that He who made them at the beginning made them male and female, and said, For this reason a man shall leave his father and mother and be joined to his wife, and the two shall become one flesh? So then, they are no longer two but*

*one flesh. **Therefore what God has joined together, let not man separate.** They said to Him, Why then did Moses command to give a certificate of divorce, and to put her away? He said to them, **Moses, because of the hardness of your hearts, permitted you to divorce your wives, but from the beginning it was not so. And I say to you, whoever divorces his wife, except for sexual immorality, and marries another, commits adultery; and whoever marries her who is divorced commits adultery.** (Matt. 19:4-9)*

*And Jesus answered and said to them, **Because of the hardness of your heart he wrote you this precept. But from the beginning of the creation, God made them male and female. For this reason a man shall leave his father and mother and be joined to his wife, and the two shall become one flesh; so then they are no longer two, but one flesh. Therefore what God has joined together, let not man separate.** (Mark 10:5-9)*

Unfortunately, at one point the divorce rate among Christians exceeded that of non-

Christians. If the husband desires to lead his marriage in the manner that has been set forth by God in scripture, he must separate himself from the world's ideas and corrupt morals and values, and embrace those values that have been set forth in the Word of God. When a marriage is based on the principles that come from the scriptures, the result is greater harmony, peace, and prosperity within the marriage and the home.

Without following these principles, both the husband and wife may try to protect themselves and their values by using defense mechanisms they learned as children. *Leading Your Marriage into the Promised Land* will show the Christian man how to lead his wife by overcoming the defense mechanisms that most commonly cause many marital problems.

In the next chapter, I will discuss the factors that can have a negative influence on marriages.

2

THE DEFENSIVE NATURE OF MARRIAGE

When a man and woman are joined together in holy matrimony, they become a family. The family is the most basic organization in society. Any organization consists of persons who have roles and responsibilities. The husband and wife also have roles and responsibilities, which classifies them as an organization.

The organization that is formed when a husband and wife are joined in marriage is typically plagued with defense mechanisms that each spouse learned during his or her childhood and as a result of negative experiences and observations in adulthood. We learn these various defense mechanisms to protect ourselves from anything that may upset, embarrass, or threaten us. We carry this defensive nature into our marriages to protect our differences in values. Organizations are plagued with defensive characteristics that can render them ineffective.

While Chris Argyris (1990) charted four factors that contribute to the defensive nature of an organization, I propose that there are five different levels that impact the defensive nature of an organization such as the family.

Figure 1 reveals that the foundation for the defensive nature of an organization begins with each person's use of *defense mechanisms* for coping.

Defense mechanisms are the unwritten rules an individual learns and utilizes to effectively deal with circumstances that are upsetting, embarrassing, or threatening.

The second level is *skilled incompetence*, which is the outcome of the defense mechanisms we have internalized. When the defensive behaviors we've learned are transformed into a learned behavior, that behavior becomes a skill – albeit an incompetent skill – that we consider necessary in order to deal with issues that are embarrassing, threatening, or upsetting. A skill that is learned from the regular application of a defense mechanism has a high degree of incompetence embedded within it, because we are unaware of how this skill will impact our future.

Skilled incompetence transforms into a *defensive routine*. Defensive routines are the third level. When the skilled incompetence is automatically exhibited at all times, the behavior is now a defensive routine.

Defensive routines lead to *fancy footwork*. Fancy footwork is the fourth level. Fancy footwork happens when individuals try to deny the behavioral inconsistencies they exhibit, or else they place blame on other people, which results in distancing themselves from taking responsibility for their behavioral inconsistencies.

Fancy footwork leads to *organizational malaise*. Organizational malaise is the final level. During this phase the individuals in the organization – which in a family includes the husband, wife, and children – will seek to find fault within the organization rather than accept responsibility for their actions and correct their behavior accordingly. The individual continues the process by accentuating the negative and deemphasizing the positive in an effort to cover up their actions. The organizational malaise is further exacerbated by a refusal of one or all the members to discuss their area of responsibility.

The Defensive Nature of Marriage

Figure 1: Levels of the Defensive Nature of an Organization

Organizational Malaise
Fancy Footwork
Defensive Routines
Skilled Incompetence
Defensive Mechanisms

Let's take a look at how the defensive nature of an organization can impact a family.

It is an acceptable fact that most boys devote more time to sports and leisure activities such as looking at television or playing video games than do girls.

If a parent chooses to follow this assumption with the reasoning of, "that's just what boys do," then that parent might allow the boys to spend all their time playing sports instead of demanding that they also do their fair share of household chores.

The Defensive Nature of Marriage

For simplicity, let's say that a family has one daughter, Shelly, and one son, Joseph, who plays basketball. Instead of Joseph being required to do household chores as his sister Shelly must do, he is allowed to practice basketball during all his free time so that he will not feel any embarrassment when involved in competition against other boys. This is a defensive mechanism. The defensive mechanism results in Joseph becoming skillfully incompetent. Joseph will play or practice basketball instead of doing household chores, supposedly as a way to improve his basketball skills. He is technically incompetent, because he is unaware that the parent's intention is to ensure that he avoids embarrassment on the basketball court, and Joseph is unaware of how this learned behavior will impact his future.

Now let's supposed that Joseph's parent begins to request that he do some chores as every member of the family does; his natural response will be that he needs to practice basketball so that he can improve his basketball skills. The behavior becomes a defensive routine.

The parent accepts the response and does not hold Joseph responsible for doing all of his assigned chores. Throughout his childhood and teen years, Joseph continues to do nothing but play basketball until one day when the parent returns from a very hard day at work and becomes angry because the dishes are not washed. The following is the ensuing dialogue that takes place between Joseph, his mother, and his sister Shelly.

Mom: *Why are these dishes not washed?*

Shelly: *It's not **my** turn to do the dishes.*

Joseph: *I had basketball practice today, so I didn't have time. Shelly normally does the dishes when I have basketball practice.*

Joseph has refused to take responsibility for his behavior and has effectively blamed his sister. This is an example of fancy footwork. Fancy footwork leads to organizational malaise. Now let's finish the example. The mother has left the scene and does not hold the son responsible for the behavior that the son has learned, which began as a defense mechanism and resulted in fancy footwork.

Now let's continue the conversation between Joseph and Shelly.

Shelly: *Why do I always have to do your chores?*

The Defensive Nature of Marriage

Joseph*: Why did you try to get me in trouble? When I have basketball practice you know the dishes are your job.*

Shelly*: Next time you're going to wash the dishes yourself whether you have basketball practice or not.*

Joseph*: You're not my boss! You don't tell me what to do! Leave me alone! I don't want to talk to you anymore!*

Shelly*: Why? I didn't do anything wrong.*

Joseph*: Leave me alone!*

The brother's response has accentuated the negative rather than the positive. He has continued the cover-up by refusing to continue the conversation, thus effectively making the cover-up a topic that is closed for discussion.

While this is a simplified example, we can see how the scenario unfolded: it began with a defense mechanism and resulted in organizational malaise.

Now let's take a look at how this defensive mechanism can impact a marriage. Remember that Joseph's mother allowed Joseph to play basketball instead of doing chores (a defense mechanism that devolved into a defensive routine).

Joseph is now a grown man and is married to Rashae. Joseph plays basketball on Saturdays while Rashae spends the day cleaning up the house. As this pattern continues Rashae becomes upset with Joseph's lack of participation in the smooth running of their home, and she decides to confront Joseph. The following dialogue ensues:

Rashae: I cleaned the whole house today and I'm exhausted. I tried to call you on your cellphone but I couldn't find you.

Joseph: You know that I play basketball every Saturday.

Rashae: Well, I need for you to help me with the housework on Saturdays.

Joseph: I don't know why I have to do housework. Isn't that a woman's job? At least, that's how it was in my home. My sister always did it. She and my mom knew how important it was for me to play basketball. Why can't you see that?

Rashae: Well, the reality is this: cleaning the house is both of our jobs!

The Defensive Nature of Marriage

Joseph: During the week you pick up my clothes off the floor and clean the kitchen, and that doesn't seem to bother you. So why are you getting on my case about cleaning on Saturdays?

Rashae: Okay ... but if you are not going to help me out, then I want a maid.

Joseph: You know that we cannot afford a maid! This is the end of this conversation!

As you can see, Joseph has avoided his responsibility in helping with the household chores, he has placed the blame on his wife, and he has emphasized that she is the blame. He ended the conversation by making the problem closed for discussion. As you can see, the defense mechanisms we learn as children can have a definite impact on our marriages.

Before we go any further let's take a look at Joseph's thinking. Argyris and Schon (1974) developed a left-hand column activity that enables individuals to redevelop and improve their behavior that results from defense mechanisms. To use this process you draw a line vertically down the center of a blank piece of paper. At the top of the left-hand column you write *What I was thinking*. Above the right-hand column you write *What was actually said.*

Below is an example of what the paper would look like if we filled in the right-hand column from our previous dialogue between Joseph and Rashae.

What I was thinking	What was actually said
	Rashae: *I cleaned the whole house today and I'm exhausted. I tried to call you on your cellphone but I couldn't find you.*
	Joseph: *You know that I play basketball every Saturday.*
	Rashae: *Well, I need for you to help me with the housework on Saturdays.*
	Joseph: *I don't know why I have to do housework. Isn't that a woman's job? At least, that's how it was in my home. My sister always did it. She and my mom knew how important it was for me to play basketball. Why can't you see that?*
	Rashae: *Well, the reality is this: cleaning the house is both of our jobs!*
	Joseph: *During the week you pick up my clothes off the floor and clean the kitchen and that doesn't seem to bother you. So why are you getting on my case about cleaning on Saturdays?*
	Rashae: *Okay ... but if you are not going to help me out, then I want a maid.*
	Joseph: *You know that we cannot afford a maid! This is the end of this conversation!*

Now let's look at what Joseph might write in the left-hand column.

What I was thinking	What was actually said
You know how to reach me.	**Rashae**: *I cleaned the whole house today and I'm exhausted. I tried to call you on your cellphone but I couldn't find you.*
I love playing basketball. I am free to do whatever I want.	**Joseph**: *You know that I play basketball every Saturday.*
That is not going to happen.	**Rashae**: *Well, I need for you to help me with the housework on Saturdays.*
Didn't your mother train you right?	**Joseph**: *I don't know why I have to do housework. Isn't that a woman's job? At least, that's how it was in my home. My sister always did it. She and my mom knew how important it was for me to play basketball. Why can't you see that?*
You must be kidding!!	**Rashae**: *Well, the reality is this: cleaning the house is both of our jobs!*
I am going to slick my way out of this one.	**Joseph**: *During the week you pick up my clothes off the floor and clean the kitchen and that doesn't seem to bother you. So why are you getting on my case about cleaning on Saturdays?*
Yeah, right. You must be crazy.	**Rashae**: *Okay ... but if you are not going to help me out, then I want a maid.*
Leave me alone so that I can watch some TV.	**Joseph**: *You know that we cannot afford a maid! This is the end of this conversation!*

As you can see, the turning point for the conversation was when Rashae told Joseph that she needed him to help with the housework. At that point in their conversation, Joseph had the opportunity to overcome his well-developed defense mechanisms and focus the conversation in a positive direction.

Now I want you to take a moment and use the left-hand column activity to evaluate your most recent argument with your wife. Think of a time when you and your wife had a really heated argument. Get a piece of paper and draw a line down the center. At the top of the left-hand column write *What I was thinking*. On the right-hand column write *What was actually said*. Next, fill in the right side completely based on what you can remember from the discussion. This will be easier to do if it was a recent discussion. If you need more rows then use additional blank papers. Next, fill in the left side. Take a look at your thinking and determine the point in the conversation when you had the opportunity to keep the conversation from becoming an argument.

Now that we have defined the different levels of the defensive nature of an organization such as the family, and we have looked at a few examples as well as evaluated our thinking during the defensive nature process, we will look at a few biblical examples that began with defensive routines and resulted in a cover-up.

A biblical example of a cover-up that resulted from the defensive nature of an organization was when Reuben and his brothers told their father that their brother Joseph had been killed. Joseph's brothers had plotted to kill Joseph. Reuben convinced his brothers to place Joseph in a pit. He was planning to return later and save Joseph by himself, but he became embarrassed when he returned to the pit and found that Joseph was gone. Reuben covered up his embarrassment by agreeing with his brothers to further cover up (to their father) what had happened to Joseph by killing a goat and dipping Joseph's coat in the goat's blood. It was also a threat to the brothers if they decided to tell Joseph's father the truth. So they returned to their father and told him that an evil beast had killed Joseph.

> *And Reuben returned unto the pit; and, behold, Joseph was not in the pit; and he rent his clothes. And he returned unto his brethren, and said, The child is not; and I, whither shall go? And they took Joseph's coat, and killed a kid of the goats, and dipped the coat in the blood; And they sent*

> *the coat of many colours, and they brought it to their father; and said, This have we found: know now whether it be thy son's coat or no. And he knew it, and said, It is my son's coat; an evil beast hath devoured him; Joseph is without doubt rent in pieces. (Genesis 37:29-33)*

The biblical story of David and Bathsheba is another example of a cover-up that results from the defensive nature of an organization. David attempted to cover up his adulterous relationship with Bathsheba (2 Samuel 11:3-27) (See appendix for entire scripture). King David observed Bathsheba taking a bath from the roof top of his castle and decided that he wanted an intimate encounter with Bathsheba, which resulted in her pregnancy. David initially attempted to cover up his infidelity by having Bathsheba's husband return home from battle. David was hoping that Uriah the Hittite would return home to Bathsheba and have relations with her so that Uriah would believe that the baby was his. David assumed this would enable him to escape from any blame that might be placed on him. David's plan did not work (because God had other plans), and he decided to take it a step further and cover up his infidelity by having Bathsheba's husband killed.

The Defensive Nature of Marriage

The family is one of the most basic organizations in our society. However, the husband and wife bring values to the relationship that will ultimately contribute to the defensive nature of the family. The husband must use a leadership style that will enable him to lead his marriage without the adverse affects that begin with defense mechanisms and result in organizational malaise.

In the next chapter, I will discuss the role that teamwork plays in the husband leading his marriage into the Promised Land.

TEAMWORK

During biblical times there was a remarkable difference in the way that pagans and Christians viewed marriage. Pagan husbands dominated their wives by treating them as inferior. Christian husbands treated their wives as persons of equal value and worth.

Likewise, Christian husbands today who treat their wives with love and respect are following the marriage plan outlined by God. God intended for the Christian husband to take on the leadership role in the marriage to ensure peace, joy, prosperity, and harmony for both the husband and the wife. Mutually they have the responsibility to love and care for one another, and doing so requires them to operate as a team. God intended for the husband and wife to operate as a team to fulfill the purpose that He has designed for their marriage.

Teamwork

Teamwork fulfills an organization's visions and goals by providing people an opportunity to work together, which enables them to attain exceptional results. Teamwork provides several advantages for Christians. For example, Jesus sent His disciples out two by two, which afforded them an opportunity to work as a team.

> *After these things the Lord appointed other seventy also, and sent them two and two before his face into every city and place, whither he himself would come. (Luke 10:1)*

Teamwork between the Christian husband and wife provides opportunities for encouragement in times of rejection. Christian husbands and wives have to report to their respective work places on a daily basis. Work can become mentally and physically draining, as well as exhausting. Encouragement from his or her spouse can be the breath of fresh air necessary to continue in the purpose that God has intended for the husband and wife.

Teamwork ensures that the combined efforts of a few results in the success of many. The biblical story in the book of Nehemiah provides an example of how teamwork results in success. Nehemiah was able to develop plans to rebuild the walls of Jerusalem even though

Teamwork

the people were discouraged.

> *Then said unto them, Ye see the
> distress that we are in, how Jerusalem
> lieth waste, and the gates thereof are
> burned with fire: come, and let us build
> up the wall of Jerusalem, that we be no
> more a reproach. Then I told them of the
> hand of my God which was good upon
> me; as also the king's words that he had
> spoken unto me. And they said, Let us
> rise up and build. So they strengthened
> their hands for this good work.
> (Nehemiah 2:17-18)*

Nehemiah called the people of Israel together
and convinced them that they could successfully
rebuild the wall as a team. Teaming together
guarantees greater success on any task. When a
husband and wife operate as a team they will have
greater success in accomplishing the purpose
God has intended for their marriage.

Teamwork ensures that the individual efforts of
each team member are extended. Peter and Paul
both set a good example of how teamwork
extends the efforts of each team member. In 1
Peter 2:4-5 Peter describes Christ as the
cornerstone and each individual believer as a
stone. In Ephesians 4:15-16, Paul describes the
body as the church and Christ as the head of the

church. Each component is vital to the successful attainment of the purpose that God has set forth for the team.

> *To whom coming, as unto a living stone, disallowed indeed of men, but chosen of God, and precious, ye also, as lively stones, are built up a spiritual house, an holy priesthood, to offer up spiritual sacrifices, acceptable to God by Jesus Christ. (1 Peter 2:4-5)*

> *But speaking the truth in love, may grow up into him in all things, which is the head, even Christ: From whom the whole body fitly joined together and compacted by that which every joint supplieth, according to the effectual working in the measure of every part, maketh increase of the body unto the edifying of itself in love. (Ephesians 4:15-16)*

The husband and wife are both vital components in the marriage when it comes to guaranteeing that they will accomplish the goals God intends for them.

Husbands and wives who operate as a team have greater opportunities to communicate their most important values. However, many husbands believe that their wives have too many criticisms about them. Husbands, please keep this important truth in mind: Wives criticize what they care about. Consider this scripture from the book of Matthew:

> *When he was set down on the judgment seat, his wife sent unto him, saying, Have thou nothing to do with that just man: for I have suffered many things this day in a dream because of him. (Matthew 27:19)*

Some typical criticisms wives have of their husbands may include:

- You don't share your feelings with me.
- Why can't you clean up behind yourself?

The criticism challenges that influence a marriage remind me of a discussion I once had with one of my former pastors. We were in our monthly men's meeting, and I asked my pastor, "Why do things always go well before a man gets married, but after the wedding the wife complains so much?" My pastor led me to Genesis 3:16. He said it was because of the way God designed the wife:

Teamwork

> *Unto the woman he said, I will greatly multiply thy sorrow and thy conception; in sorrow thou shalt bring forth children; and thy desire shall be to thy husband, and he shall rule over thee. (Genesis 3:16)*

One of the important points is that God made the wife to have her desire for her husband. God designed a man's wife to have a commitment to her husband. If your wife points out that the grass is too high, then she has a commitment to have a house that looks as appealing on the outside as she most likely keeps it on the inside. If your wife is concerned about the finances, then she has a commitment to financial security.

Take a few minutes to evaluate your wife's commitments. Take a sheet of paper and divide it into two columns. Write down in the left column recent concerns that your wife may have voiced. Now, line by line, evaluate your wife's commitments as they relate to each concern. In the right-hand column write down "My wife is committed to ..." and fill in the blank.

The next time you hear one of her concerns you can respond by saying "Honey, I am happy that you are committed to ..." and continue the discussion on how to address the concern or solve the problem. Now you and your wife can continue your day in happiness and not strife.

I would complete the previous examples as follows:

Criticism	Commitment
When he was set down on the judgment seat, his wife sent unto him, saying, Have thou nothing to do with that just man: for I have suffered many things this day in a dream because of him. (Matthew 27:19)	My wife is committed to my safety
You don't share your feelings with me.	My wife is committed to communicating with me.
Why can't you clean up behind yourself?	My wife is committed to a clean house.

Teamwork provides a vehicle that increases marital bliss between a husband and wife. When a husband and wife work together they can attain exceptional results. Teamwork increases communication, which ensures their success in attaining the vision that God has set forth for their marriage.

In the next chapter, I will discuss the role that shared vision plays in the husband leading his marriage into the Promised Land.

SHARED VISION

A shared vision is a mental image that two or more persons agree on. A shared vision provides the focus and energy necessary for the husband and wife to begin the learning process necessary for the development and fulfillment of their family goals. Husbands and wives will no longer consider only their individual needs but will work together to meet their family's needs and wants, as well as each other's desires.

Shared vision is a powerful tool that unites any family or organization. The tower of Babel is a biblical example that shows the power of a shared vision and then what happens when that vision is lost through a breakdown in communication. During biblical times, after the flood, the people of the city of Babel decided to build a great tower. They developed a shared vision, which resulted in the construction of a tower that would go to the heavens. The people decided to build the tower to promote man instead of God. God decided that the focus of the shared vision was corrupt. He had a different plan for man entering into heaven and stopped the building of the tower by causing the people to speak different languages.

> *And the whole earth was of one language, and of one speech. And it came to pass, as they journeyed from the east, that they found a plain in the land of Shinar; and they dwelt there. And they said one to another, Go to, let us make brick, and burn them thoroughly. And they had brick for stone, and slime had they for mortar. And they said, Go to, let us build us a city and a tower, whose top may reach unto heaven; and let us make us a name, lest we be scattered abroad upon the face of the whole earth. And the LORD came down to see the city and the tower, which the children of men builded. And the LORD said, Behold, the people is one, and they have all one language; and this they begin to do: and now nothing will be restrained from them, which they have imagined to do. Go to, let us go down, and there confound their language, that they*

> *may not understand one another's speech. So the LORD scattered them abroad from thence upon the face of all the earth: and they left off to build the city. Therefore is the name of it called Babel; because the LORD did there confound the language of all the earth: and from thence did the LORD scatter them abroad upon the face of all the earth. (Genesis 11:1-9)*

Shared visions give enormous power to the people in the organization who are part of that vision. Jesus has guaranteed that when an organization of at least two people, such as a husband and wife, come together in agreement, He will be with them.

> **Again I say unto you, That if two of you shall agree on earth as touching any thing that they shall ask, it shall be done for them of my Father which is in heaven. For where two or three are gathered together in my name, there am I in the midst of them.** *(Matthew 18:19)*

Imagine the power and comfort your marriage will have after you and your wife complete the process of creating a shared vision. The two of you will become a united team, and you will experience a marriage founded on biblical values and principles. When organizations such as a husband and wife team develop a shared vision directed towards glorifying God, the possibilities are heavenly.

In the next chapter, I will outline the entire process required to lead your marriage into the Promised Land.

LEADING YOUR MARRIAGE

Leading your marriage begins with you and your wife developing a shared vision with the Holy Scriptures as its foundation. The Holy Scriptures reveal that without a vision we will perish.

> *Where there is no vision, the people perish. (Proverbs 29:18)*

After developing your shared vision, you and your wife will work as a team to develop goals in the areas listed on the next page.

> Spiritual
> Family
> Social
> Educational
> Physical
> Employment/Work
> Recreation/Fun
> Financial

Establishing goals in each area will ensure that you and your wife have clearly defined your desires for your marriage. Some may argue that having goals is ungodly. The scriptures reveal, however, that God is goal-oriented. One of God's goals for us is to become more like Him.

> *Beloved, now are we the sons of God, and it doth not yet appear what we shall be: but we know that, when he shall appear, we shall be like him; for we shall see him as he is. (1 John 3:2)*

The scriptures support the development of goals.

> *Know ye not that they which run in a race run all, but one receiveth the prize? So run, that ye may obtain. And every man that striveth for the mastery is temperate in all things. Now they do it to obtain a corruptible crown; but we*

> *an incorruptible. (1 Corinthians 9:24-25)*

You and your wife will develop spiritual and natural goals. Spiritual goals will create a holy marriage that glorifies God. Spiritual goals are the most important goals in a marriage. Spiritual goals developed by a man and his wife will provide the motivation to fulfill their spiritual lives. Lack of spiritual goals is a primary reason why so many married couples have challenges in their marriages. Without spiritual goals, married couples will have difficulty accomplishing the purposes for which God brought them together as one.

Aside from spiritual goals, there are natural goals that need to be set, as these will also influence your marriage. Natural goals for Christians result from the necessity to exist and interact in the world. The Holy Scriptures reveal that husbands need to know their wives' needs, which includes the goals they have for themselves and their family.

> *Likewise, ye husbands, dwell with them according to knowledge, giving honour unto the wife, as unto the weaker vessel, and as being heirs together of the grace of life; that your prayers be not hindered. (1 Peter 3:7)*

Let's examine the separate goals that you and your wife will accomplish during a seven-week period.

Week 1:

To begin the process, you will need markers and easel paper. I recommend using washable markers. At the top of the easel paper write *Most Important Values*. Next, draw a line down the center of the paper. Write your name at the top of one side and your wife's name at the top of the other side. Place the easel paper on a hallway wall that you and your wife have to pass by daily. (This works well if you use the easel paper that sticks like a post-it note, but when taken off the wall won't leave a mark.) Place the markers in a place where you and your wife will have access to it when you need it. If you have children or other family members in the house, place the easel paper in your bedroom. This is a private matter between you and your wife. Now, for one week, you and your wife will write down underneath your names your most important marriage values.

Leading Your Marriage

Your easel paper should look like the following example:

Most Important Values

Husband's Name	Wife's Name

You and your wife are not allowed to discuss what is written down until your scheduled meeting at the end of the week. Remember when I discussed the defensive nature of a marriage? The husband and wife bring different defense mechanisms to the marriage, which can result in blame-placing and cover-up. By waiting until the scheduled meeting to discuss what is written down, you give yourself and your wife an opportunity to reflect on what is written without encountering the adverse influences that result from the defensive nature of a marriage. **This will be the rule for each individual goal setting activity during each of the next seven weeks.** Make sure that you and your wife agree on a date and time for the next meeting.

Week 2:

Below is an example of what a husband and wife might write on the easel paper:

Most Important Values

Husband	Wife
Trust	Integrity
Integrity	Loyalty
Honesty	Generosity
Loyalty	Respect
Influence	Dependability
Enjoyment	Honesty

You may have noticed there are three areas that the husband and wife agree on in this example. The three areas are integrity, loyalty, and honesty. Because these three areas are important to both spouses, they become the foundation for the marriage, the cornerstone from which the marriage is built as the husband continues to lead their marriage into the Promised Land. Of course, you and your wife might agree on more than three values.

When the day comes for your agreed-upon weekly meeting, begin by circling the values that you and your wife agree on. Now take another sheet of easel paper, and you and your wife write down what each value means to you. You and your wife may use a dictionary to remind you of the deeper meanings of each word. Take this sheet of easel paper and place it alongside the first one. In the example there were three areas of agreement; therefore, you would need three more pieces of blank easel paper. You will need a blank sheet of easel paper for each area of agreement. Write down each agreed-upon term at the top of each separate paper. Draw a line down the center of each sheet of easel paper. Write your name on one side and your wife's name on the other side. The homework assignment is for you and your wife to write down how you will demonstrate the agreed-upon values in your marriage.

Below and on the next page are examples of the three blank easel papers for our previous example.

Integrity

Husband Name	Wife Name

Honesty

Husband Name	Wife Name

Loyalty

Husband Name	Wife Name

Also, you and you wife are responsible for individually finding scriptures that define each value. Your first meeting is now over. **Remember, you and your wife are not allowed to discuss what was written down until your scheduled meeting at the end of the next week.** Also, don't consider each meeting to be closed until you have ended with a loving embrace and reminded each other of how much you love and are appreciative of one another!

Week 3:

During this meeting you and your wife will develop a shared vision. The first step is to share the scriptures that each of you found during the previous week. You and your wife will now choose one scripture for each value that was agreed upon in week two. Once you have agreed on the scriptures and chosen the ones that mean the most to you, the next thing you will do is to develop a shared vision. The objective is to combine the agreed-upon values into one statement.

Here are a few vision statement starters:
- Our vision is to ...
- We envision a marriage that is ...
- Our marriage will be known for ...
- Our marriage values and beliefs will be reflected by ...
- We will effectively build a marriage that ...
- We will create a marriage that ...
- Our marriage will celebrate ...

The following is a vision statement for the given example:

> "Our vision is to faithfully commit to walk in honesty, integrity, and loyalty towards one another as we walk before God."

To summarize once again, the vision statement is a statement that includes all of the values that you and your wife agree on. Take a blank sheet of easel paper and write the agreed-upon vision on it.

Now that you and your wife have developed an agreed-upon shared vision, your homework is to memorize the agreed-upon scriptures and the shared vision statement. During the next meeting the husband will recite the scriptures and vision statement to the wife, and the wife will recite the scriptures and vision statement to the husband.

Next, you will need three separate sheets of blank easel paper. On the top of one paper write *Spiritual*. Draw a line down the middle. Write your name on one side and your wife's name on the other side. On the top of the next paper write *Family*. Write your name on one side and your wife's name on the other side. On the final paper write *Social*. Write your name on one side and your wife's name on the other side. On the next page are examples of the three easel papers:

Leading Your Marriage

Spiritual

Husband Name	Wife Name

Family

Husband Name	Wife Name

Social

Husband Name	Wife Name

Place the papers in the designated area. For this week, you and your wife will write your goals for these areas. For the paper titled *Spiritual*, you and your wife will write down your spiritual goals. For the paper titled *Family*, you and your wife will write down the specific goals you hope to accomplish in your family. For the paper titled *Social*, you and your wife will write down your social goals, which includes how the husband wants to interact with his wife, how the wife wants to interact with her husband, how the husband wants his wife to interact with him, how the wife wants her husband to interact with her, and how the husband and wife want to interact with their extended family and friends. As before, place the easel papers, along with the previous papers, in their designated location. **Remember, you and your wife are not allowed to discuss what was written down until your scheduled meeting at the end of the next week.**

Week 4:

During this meeting you and your wife will begin by reciting the scriptures and shared vision statement to one another. Next, you and your wife will review the easel papers titled *Spiritual*, *Family*, and *Social*. Remember, your primary objective is to develop three agreed-upon goals for each area. On the next page is an example of an easel paper that contains a couple's spiritual goals:

Spiritual

Husband Name	Wife Name
Attend church once a week	Weekly family prayer
Weekly family bible study	Daily Bible reading
Family Holy Communion once a month	Attend church twice a week
Daily prayer	Increase giving
Weekly family prayer	Daily prayer
Increase tithing and giving	

As you can see from the example, the husband and wife agree on two goals. Now the husband and wife will work as a team to agree on one final goal.

If you reach a point of impasse or deadlock, then go back to the agreed-upon shared vision and make sure that your goals are consistent with your shared vision.

Note: If you and your wife have no goals in common, then together you and your wife will select three goals to agree on and accomplish.

Once you and your wife have agreed on three goals, write each goal on a separate sheet of easel paper. Write down the area of agreement first and then your shared goals underneath it.

Now you will prepare for the next meeting. You will need three separate sheets of blank easel paper. On the top of one paper write *Educational*. Draw a line down the center. Write your name on one side and your wife's name on the other side. On the top of the next paper write *Physical*. Write your name on one side and your wife's name on the other side. On the final paper write *Employment/Work*. Write your name on one side and your wife's name on the other side. As before, place the easel papers, along with the previous papers, in the designated location.

For this week, you and your wife will write your goals for these areas. For the paper titled *Educational*, you and your wife will write down any goals you may have for continuing your education. For the paper titled *Physical*, you and your wife will write down the goals you have for meeting your physical needs. Physical goals can include what you and your wife will do to remain physically attractive to each other, what you will do to remain healthy, what sort of exercise plan you want to build into your daily lives, and so on. For the paper titled *Employment/Work*, you and your wife will write down your employment/work goals. **Remember, you and your wife are not allowed to discuss what has been written down until your scheduled meeting at the end of the next week.**

On the next two pages are examples of the three blank easel papers:

Educational

Husband Name	Wife Name

Physical

Husband Name	Wife Name

Employment/Work

Husband Name	Wife Name

Week 5:

You and your wife will begin the meeting this week by reciting to one another the scriptures and vision statement you agreed on previously. Next, you and your wife will review the easel papers with the headings of *Educational*, *Physical*, and *Employment/Work*. The goal for this week is to develop three agreed-upon goals for each area. On the next page is an example of an easel paper filled in with a couple's physical goals.

Physical

Husband's Name	Wife's Name
Keep hair neatly trimmed	Lose weight
Walk after work	Beauty treatments
Grow a beard	Change diet
Lose weight	Walk five times a week
Eat less meat	

As you can see from the example on this page, the husband and wife agree on one goal – to lose weight. Now the husband and wife will work as a team to agree on two more goals.

If you reach a point of impasse or deadlock, then go back to the agreed-upon shared vision and make sure that the goals are consistent with that vision.

Note: If you and your wife have no goal in common, then together you and your wife will select three goals that you agree on.

Once you and your wife have reached an agreement, write the goals down on a separate easel paper. Write down each area of agreement first and then the pertinent goals underneath.

Now you will prepare for the next meeting. You will need two separate sheets of blank easel paper. At the top of one easel paper write *Recreation/Fun*. Draw a line down the center of the paper. Write your name on one side and your wife's name on the other side. On the top of the next paper write *Financial*. Write your name on one side and your wife's name on the other side. For the paper titled *Recreation/Fun*, you and your wife will write down goals you have for your family's recreation/fun time and the goals you have for just the two of you. For the paper titled *Financial*, you and your wife will write down your financial goals. As before, place the easel papers, along with the previous papers, in the designated location. Throughout the week, you and your wife will individually write your goals for these areas. **Remember, you and your wife are not allowed to discuss what has been written down until your scheduled meeting at the end of the week.**

On the next page are examples of the two blank easel papers:

Recreational/Fun

Husband Name	Wife Name

Financial

Husband Name	Wife Name

Week 6:

This week you and your wife will begin the meeting by reciting your chosen scriptures and shared vision statement to one another. Next, you and your wife will review the easel papers titled *Recreation/Fun* and *Financial*. The goal is to develop three agreed-upon goals for each area.

Below is an example of an easel paper filled in with a couple's recreation/fun goals:

Recreation/Fun

Husband Name	Wife Name
Play on baseball team	Cardio vascular exercises
Vacation	Sex
Sex	Swim
Weight-lifting	Vacation
Run in marathon	Play on softball team

As you can see from the example on this page, the husband and wife agree on two goals – sexual intimacy and taking vacations. Now the husband and wife will work together as a team to agree on a final goal.

If you and your wife reach a point of impasse or deadlock, go back to the agreed-upon shared vision and make sure the goals you've set are consistent with that vision.

Note: If you and your wife have no goal in common, then the two of you will together select three goals that you both want to meet.

Once you and your wife have reached an agreement, write the goals down on a separate sheet of easel paper. Write down each area first and the corresponding goals underneath those areas. Now you will schedule a meeting for the final week.

Week 7/Final week:

During this meeting you and your wife will begin by reciting your chosen scriptures and shared vision statement to one another. Next, you and your wife will review each agreed-upon goal and make a timeline. A timeline can include when you will meet an agreed-upon financial goal. Or you could agree on dinner out twice a month, if this was one of your social goals. Every goal must have an agreed-upon time line for completion or repetition.

On the next page is an example of a chart filled in with a couple's agreed-upon goals and their corresponding timelines.

Area	Goal	Timeline
Spiritual		
	Family prayer	Weekly
	Church attendance	Twice a week
	Tithing and giving	Every paycheck
Physical		
	Beauty treatments	Twice a month
	Walking	Three times a week
	Lose weight	Ongoing
Recreation/Fun		
	Vacation	Twice a year
	Sex	Twice a week
	Baseball/Softball	Seasonal

On the next page is an example of a blank template for all the areas.

Area	Goal	Timeline
Spiritual		
Family		
Social		
Educational		
Physical		
Employment/Work		
Recreation/Fun		
Financial		

Now that you and your wife have completed the process, there is one task left to accomplish. Before we go further, let's review what you and your wife have accomplished as a team:

> Spiritual goals (founded on the Holy Scriptures)
> At least three family goals
> At least three social goals
> At least three educational goals
> At least three physical goals
> At least three employment/work goals

>   At least three recreation/fun goals
>   At least three financial goals

You and your wife have also completed timelines for each goal.

Now you and your wife will determine a budgeted dollar amount for each goal. Finally, compare the budget for your goals to your family budget. If you and your wife find that your goals exceed your financial budget, then you and your wife will need to agree on what goals to prioritize.

You and your wife will also need to agree on when you'll have your next meeting to review completion of your goals. I recommend meeting every three months to review your goals. If necessary, redo the process.

NEW BEGINNINGS

Now that you've come through this seven-week journey together, your marriage now has a new direction – one that you and your wife have both agreed on together.

In the biblical times, the husband was the supreme authority and the wife looked at the husband as her lord.

> *Therefore Sarah laughed within herself, saying, After I am waxed old shall I have pleasure, my lord being old also? (Genesis 18:12)*

Society's changing social and economic value systems have changed the values that influence the Christian husband and wife, which ultimately influences the Christian marriage. Society has made it increasingly difficult for the husband to step into his rightful role as the priest and lord of his family. By leading your wife into the promised land of your marriage, you have used a leadership style that provides not only the opportunity for you and your wife to become a team with a shared vision that God intended for your marriage, but you have also taken your rightful place as the leader and priest in the family. The best part of all is that you have done this without alienating your wife because the two of you have been in agreement every step of the way.

> *Likewise, ye husbands, dwell with them according to knowledge, giving honour unto the wife, as unto the weaker vessel, and as being heirs together of the grace of life; that your prayers be not hindered. (1Peter3:7)*

Your marriage can be a living example of these eternal words.

References

Amato, P., & Rogers, S. (1997). A Longitudinal Study of Marital Problems and Subsequent Divorce. *Journal of Marriage and the Family, 59*(3), 612-624.

Argyris, C. (1990). Overcoming Organizational Defenses: Facilitating Organizational Learning. Upper Saddle River, New Jersey: Prentice Hall

Argyris, C., & Schon, D. (1974). *Theory in Practice: Increasing professional effectiveness.* Boston: Allyn and Bacon.

Bienvenu, M. (1970). Measurement of Marital Coordinator. *The Family Coordinator, 19*(1), 26-31.

Haeberle, E. (1981). *The Sex Atlas.* New York: The Continuum Publishing Company.

Kearney, P. (1984). Perceptual discrepancies in teacher communication style. *Communication, 13*, 5-108.

Kegan, R., & Lahey, L. (2001). *How the Way We Talk Can Change the Way We Work: Seven Languages for Transformation.* San Francisco, CA: Jossey-Bass.

Matthews, V. (1991). *Manners and Customs in the Bible: An Illustrated Guide to Daily Life in Bible Times.* Peabody, Massachusetts: Hendrickson Publishers, Inc.

Quickverse, (1999). Hiawatha, IA: Parsons Technology.

Schakelford, T. (1998). Divorce as a consequence of spousal infidelity. In V. de Munck (Ed.), *Romantic love and sexual behaviors* (pp. 135-153). Westport, CT: Praeger.

Senge, P. (1990). *The Fifth Discipline: The Art and Practice of the Learning Organization.* New York: Doubleday.

Women of Spirit. (2009). In *Wives' Top Complaints About Husbands.* Retrieved January 9, 2009, from http://www.womenofspirit.com/index.php?id=147:

Leading Your Marriage into the Promised Land
Step by Step

Equipment Needed: Washable Markers
Easel Pad

Week 1:	
Step 1:	At the top of the easel paper write "Most Important Values"
Step 2:	Next, draw a line down the middle.
Step 3:	Write your name on one side and your wife's name on the other side.
Step 4:	Place the easel paper on a hallway or bedroom wall that you and your wife pass by daily.
Step 5:	Place the marker in a place where you and your wife will have access to the marker when you need it.
Step 6:	You and your wife will write down underneath your name the most important marriage values.

Week 2:	
Step 1:	Begin the meeting by circling the values that you and your wife agree on.
Step 2:	Write down each agreed-upon value at the top of each separate easel paper.
Step 3:	Draw a line down the middle of the easel paper.
Step 5:	Write your name on one side and your wife's name on the other side.
Step 5:	The homework assignment is for you and your wife to write down how you will demonstrate the agreed-upon values in a marriage.
Step 6:	You and you wife are responsible for finding Holy Bible scriptures that define each value.

Week 3:	
Step 1:	Share the scriptures that each of you found during the previous week.
Step 2:	You and your wife will now agree on a scripture for each value that was agreed-upon in week two.
Step 3:	You and your wife will now develop a shared vision.
Step 4:	Take an easel paper and write the agreed-upon vision on it.
Step 5:	Memorize the agreed-upon scriptures and the vision statement for the next meeting.
Step 6:	Get three separate blank easel papers.
Step 7:	On the top of one paper write "Spiritual".
Step 8:	Draw a line down the middle.
Step 9:	Write your name on one side and your wife's name on the other side.
Step 10:	On the top of the next paper write "Family".
Step 11:	Write your name on one side and your wife's name on the other side.
Step 12:	On the final paper write "Social".

Week 3: (Continued)	
Step 13:	Write your name on one side and your wife's name on the other side.
Step 14:	Place the papers in the designated area.
Step 15:	For this week you and your wife will write your goals for the areas.
Step 16:	For the paper titled "Spiritual" you and your wife will write down your spiritual goals.
Step 17:	For the paper titled "Family" you and your wife will write down your family goals.
Step 18:	For the paper titled "Social" you and your wife will write down your social goals.

Week 4:	
Step 1:	You and your wife will begin the meeting by reciting the scriptures and vision statement to one another.
Step 2:	You and your wife will review and develop three agreed-upon goals in the "Spiritual", "Family", and "Social" areas.
Step 3:	Once you and your wife have reached an agreement write the goals down on a separate easel paper. Write down the area first and then the goals underneath it.
Step 4:	Prepare for the next meeting.
Step 5:	Get three separate blank easel papers.
Step 6:	On the top of one paper write "Educational".
Step 7:	Draw a line down the middle.
Step 8:	Write your name on one side and your wife's name on the other side.
Step 9:	On the top of the next paper write "Physical".
Step 10:	Draw a line down the middle.

Week 4: (Continued)	
Step 11:	Write your name on one side and your wife's name on the other side.
Step 12:	On the final paper write "Employment/Work".
Step 13:	Draw a line down the middle.
Step 14:	Write your name on one side and your wife's name on the other side.
Step 15:	Place the papers in the designated area.
Step 16:	For this week you and your wife will write your goals for the areas.
Step 17:	For the paper titled "Educational" you and your wife will write down your educational goals.
Step 18:	For the paper titled "Physical" you and your wife will write down your physical goals.

Week 4: (Continued)	
Step 19:	For the paper titled "Employment/Work" you and your wife will write down your employment/work goals.

Week 5:	
Step 1:	You and your wife will begin the meeting by reciting the scriptures and vision statement to one another.
Step 2:	You and your wife will review and develop three agreed-upon goals in the "Education", "Physical", and "Employment/Work" areas.
Step 3:	Once you and your wife have reached an agreement write the goals down on a separate blank easel paper. Write down the area first and then the goal underneath it.
Step 4:	Prepare for the next meeting.
Step 5:	Get two separate blank easel papers.
Step 6:	On the top of one paper write "Recreation/Fun".
Step 7:	Draw a line down the middle.
Step 8:	Write your name on one side and your wife's name on the other side.
Step 9:	On the top of the next paper write "Financial".
Step 10:	Write your name on one side and your wife's name on the other side.

Week 5: (Continued)	
Step 11:	Place the papers in the designated area.
Step 12:	For this week you and your wife will write your goals for the areas.
Step 13:	For the paper titled "Recreation" you and your wife will write down your recreation goals.
Step 14:	For the paper titled "Financial" you and your wife will write down your financial goals.

Week 6:	
Step 1:	You and your wife will begin the meeting by reciting the scriptures and vision statement to one another.
Step 2:	You and your wife will review and develop three agreed-upon goals in the "Recreation/Fun", and "Financial" areas.
Step 3:	Once you and your wife have reached an agreement write the goals down on a separate easel paper. Write down the area first and then the goal underneath it.
Step 4:	Schedule the next meeting.
Step 5:	Place the papers in the designated area.

Week 7:	
Step 1:	You and your wife will begin the meeting by reciting the scriptures and vision statement to one another.
Step 2:	You and your wife will review each agreed-upon goal and make a time line.
Step 3:	You and your wife will determine a dollar amount for each agreed-upon goal. If you find that the goals exceed your financial budget you and your wife will have to prioritize your goals.
Step 4:	Schedule next meeting to review goal accomplishments in three months

Scripture Not in Text

2 Samuel 11:3-27

And David sent and inquired after the woman.
And one said, Is not this Bathsheba, the
daughter of Eliam, the wife of Uriah the Hittite?
And David sent messengers, and took her; and
she came in unto him, and he lay with her; for
she was purified from her uncleanness: and she
returned unto her house. And the woman
conceived, and sent and told David, and said, I
am with child.

And David sent to Joab, saying, Send me Uriah
the Hittite. And Joab sent Uriah to David. And
when Uriah was come unto him, David
demanded of him how Joab did, and how the
people did, and how the war prospered. And
David said to Uriah, Go down to thy house, and
wash thy feet. And Uriah departed out of the
king's house, and there followed him a mess of
meat from the king. But Uriah slept at the door
of the king's house with all the servants of his
lord, and went not down to his house. And when

they had told David, saying, Uriah went not down unto his house, David said unto Uriah, Camest thou not from thy journey? why then didst thou not go down unto thine house? And Uriah said unto David, The ark, and Israel, and Judah, abide in tents; and my lord Joab, and the servants of my lord, are encamped in the open fields; shall I then go into mine house, to eat and to drink, and to lie with my wife? as thou livest, and as thy soul liveth, I will not do this thing. And David said to Uriah, Tarry here to day also, and to morrow I will let thee depart. So Uriah abode in Jerusalem that day, and the morrow. And when David had called him, he did eat and drink before him; and he made him drunk: and at even he went out to lie on his bed with the servants of his lord, but went not down to his house.

And it came to pass in the morning, that David wrote a letter to Joab, and sent it by the hand of Uriah. And he wrote in the letter, saying, Set ye Uriah in the forefront of the hottest battle, and retire ye from him, that he may be smitten, and die. And it came to pass, when Joab observed the city, that he assigned Uriah unto a place where he knew that valiant men were. And the men of the city went out, and fought with Joab: and there fell some of the people of the servants of David; and Uriah the Hittite died also. Then Joab sent and told David all the things concerning the war; And charged the messenger, saying, When thou hast made an end of telling the matters of the war unto the king, And if so be that the king's wrath arise, and he say unto thee, Wherefore approached ye so nigh unto the city when ye did fight? knew ye not that they would shoot from the wall? Who smote Abimelech the son of Jerubbesheth? did not a woman cast a piece of a millstone upon him from the wall, that he died in Thebez? why went ye nigh the wall? then say thou, Thy servant Uriah the Hittite is dead also. So the messenger went, and came and showed David all that Joab had sent him for. And the messenger said unto David, Surely the men prevailed against us, and came out unto us into the field, and we were upon them even unto the entering of the gate. And the shooters shot from off the wall upon thy servants; and some of the king's servants be dead, and thy servant Uriah the Hittite is dead also. Then David said unto the messenger, Thus shalt thou say unto Joab, Let not this thing displease thee, for the sword devoureth one as well as another: make thy battle more strong against the city, and overthrow it: and encourage thou him. And when the wife of Uriah heard that Uriah her husband was dead, she mourned for her husband. And when the mourning was past, David sent and fetched her to his house, and she became his wife, and bare him a son. But the thing that David had done displeased the LORD.

About the Author

Dr. Derrick L. Campbell is the founder and Chief Executive Officer of DLC Consultant Group.

He holds a Bachelor of Science degree in Electronics Engineering Technology from Capital Institute of Technology, a second Bachelor of Science degree in Math Education from the University of the District of Columbia, a Masters in Education Administration from Lincoln University, and a doctoral degree in Educational leadership from Rowan University.

Dr. Campbell authored his first book, *Promoting Positive Racial Teacher-Student Classroom Relationships*, in January 2008. He developed a Cultural Relationship Training Program that improves teacher-student classroom relationships, which has resulted in reduced disciplinary infractions and increased student achievement. He has also developed a program that improves supervisor-employee workplace relationships as well as a leadership training program for businesses and educational institutions.

Dr. Campbell has lectured at various locations throughout the nation, including the National Association for the Advancement of Colored People (NAACP). He has ministered to the youth at his church on the topic of Christian student rights in the public schools and has ministered at a local New Jersey church on the topic of overcoming the poverty cycle. He has been a board member of the men's ministry, Athletes United in Christ, and has participated in various church activities.

Dr. Campbell has been successfully and happily married for more than nine years.

Dr. Campbell is available for speaking engagements. He can be contacted through www.dlconsultantgroup.com.

Notes

Notes

Notes

Notes

Notes

Notes

_____

_____

Notes

Notes

8480837R0

Made in the USA
Charleston, SC
13 June 2011